Millions of marriages end in divorce, leaving parents fightir
battles. Attorneys repeatedly advise their clients the impor
there was no guide on how and what to document, **until now**. *"For Children's
Sake: Journal It"* is a powerful tool that can make the difference between
knowing the opposing parent is unfit and proving it.

You no longer have to write paragraph after paragraph in a hard to follow
journal. *"For Children's Sake: Journal It"* will enable you to document quickly
while keeping organized files.

"For Children's Sake: Journal It" was created just for **YOU!** You now have a tool
to document thoroughly and with ease. There are no longer questions on what
to document and how to. **DOCUMENT, DOCUMENT, DOCUMENT!** Your
children's future is worth it.

DON'T EVER ALLOW YOUR CHILD ACCESS TO THIS BOOK!

For Children's Sake, Journal It!, January 2011

Printed in the United States of America

ISBN: 978-0-615-44169-6

Table of Contents

PHONE LOG:

Often times, parents swear to their undying commitment, involvement and love for their children in a courtroom. They boldly lie, claiming they call their children regularly. But is this the case? Document all communication with the other parent including text messages, voicemails, outgoing, incoming and missed calls.

Did you communicate to the other parent about the class play, athletic event, award ceremony or another event that was special to your child? Did they participate in the event? If not, did they call and wish your child good luck or say congratulations? Prove their lack of involvement through your documentation!

Do you receive harassing messages or phone calls? Does the other parent call at all hours? Retain all significant phone records! Use the phone log to document every call and message. **NEVER respond inappropriately as your response will also be documented!** Photograph significant text messages and staple to appropriate page. Make sure the actual phone number displays, not the name you have programmed for that number.

CHILDREN'S PICK-UP:

Did the other parent show up for the pick-up? Were they on time? Did they change the location for some reason? Or did they send another party to complete the exchange? If so, did the children know this person? How did the children react when seeing the other parent or the designated party? Were there proper car seat restraints? Were there any confrontations during the exchange? Remember never argue or fight in front of your children as this can have a devastating affect on them. Document the details of the exchange in this section.

DEPARTURE APPEARANCE:

Take a quick picture of your children minutes before the exchange. It's vital to prove your children were clean, in proper fitting clothing and free of bruises or any other marks. Write the date on the picture and staple it accordingly.

DON'T EVER ALLOW YOUR CHILD ACCESS TO THIS JOURNAL!

INSTRUCTIONS PROVIDED TO OTHER PARTY REGARDING CHILDREN:

Does your child have any special needs that require attention while in the care of the other parent? Are there any activities that your child should not be participating in due to an illness or injury? Document the instructions that you provided. If there are any bruises or injuries, document how they occurred in this section including any medical care that was provided.

CHILDREN'S RETURN

Documenting the children's return is just as important as documenting their pick-up. Who dropped off the children? Were the kids in proper car seat restraints? Was the other parent late, a no-show, or did they change the return location? Did a police report need to be filed? Are you constantly making accommodations to meet their needs?

CHILDREN'S RETURN APPEARANCE

Take a quick snapshot of the children immediately after the exchange. Are they in clean, proper fitting clothing, just as you sent them? Do they have any marks or bruises on them? Do they look like they were well taken care of? Write the date on the picture and staple it in the section provided.

VISIT DETAILS

Ask the children non-leading questions. For example: Tell me about your weekend. What did you do? Is there anything that I should know? Make your children feel comfortable talking to you. Don't make it feel like an interrogation. If you hear information that shocks you, don't let the kids know you're upset. Instead document it and contact authorities and your attorney, if necessary.

Were all of the children's belongings returned and undamaged? If not, document what was missing or damaged. Did the other parent follow the instructions to meet the children's special needs? Were any birthdays or holidays celebrated? Or did they pass without even being acknowledged? If so, document how this affected the children? Were the kids injured during the visit or sick soon after?

DON'T EVER ALLOW YOUR CHILD ACCESS TO THIS JOURNAL!

CHILDREN'S MONTHLY ACCOMPLISHMENTS:

Prove you provide a stable environment for your children. Did your children receive a great report card or interim report, an award for perfect attendance or another great academic accomplishment? Maybe, it's as simple as a hard-earned "A" on a test or quiz that they studied hours for.

Other accomplishments can include: enrollment or involvement in extra-curriculum activities including scouts, school clubs or sport teams. Well-rounded children are involved. Do you provide a stable environment for your children? Prove it!

PERIODIC PUBLIC RECORD REQUEST

Most states allow you to request public records online, by mail or by phone. These records can include 911 calls, non-emergency police responses, criminal charges and civil judgments. Requesting these reports periodically can be invaluable to your case and your children's well-being. It can prove your children are subject to an unsafe, unstable environment while in the care of the opposing parent.

Use the chart provided to summarize the reports. Also, an example of a public record request letter is included. Staple the reports that you receive in the section provided. Depending on the results, you may need to provide a copy of the reports to your attorney or to Child Services.

DON'T EVER ALLOW YOUR CHILD ACCESS TO THIS JOURNAL!

MONTH 1

PHONE LOG FOR MONTH:

DATE	CALL LENGTH	CALL TYPE	WHO CALLED	CONVERSATION DETAILS/CHILDREN'S REACTION

PHONE LOG FOR MONTH:

DATE	CALL LENGTH	CALL TYPE	WHO CALLED	CONVERSATION DETAILS/CHILDREN'S REACTION

PHONE LOG FOR MONTH:

DATE	CALL LENGTH	CALL TYPE	WHO CALLED	CONVERSATION DETAILS/CHILDREN'S REACTION

PHONE LOG FOR MONTH:

DATE	CALL LENGTH	CALL TYPE	WHO CALLED	CONVERSATION DETAILS/CHILDREN'S REACTION

ATTACH PICTURES OF SIGNIFICANT TEXT MESSAGES

ATTACH PICTURES OF SIGNIFICANT TEXT MESSAGES

ATTACH PICTURES OF SIGNIFICANT TEXT MESSAGES

CHILDREN'S PICK UP

MONTH OF:					
DATE	WHO	LATE OR NO SHOW	PICK UP ISSUES	PROPER CAR SEATS?	CHILDREN'S REACTION TO INITIATION OF VISIT

DETAILS:

DETAILS:

DETAILS:

DETAILS:

DETAILS:

CHILDREN'S PICK UP

MONTH OF:					
DATE	WHO	LATE OR NO SHOW	PICK UP ISSUES	PROPER CAR SEATS?	CHILDREN'S REACTION TO INITIATION OF VISIT

DETAILS:

DETAILS:

DETAILS:

DETAILS:

DETAILS:

CHILDREN'S PICK UP

MONTH OF:					
DATE	WHO	LATE OR NO SHOW	PICK UP ISSUES	PROPER CAR SEATS?	CHILDREN'S REACTION TO INITIATION OF VISIT

DETAILS:

DETAILS:

DETAILS:

DETAILS:

DETAILS:

FASTEN PICTURES OF CHILDREN'S DEPARTURE APPEARANCE; DATE THE BACK OF EACH PICTURE

FASTEN PICTURES OF CHILDREN'S DEPARTURE APPEARANCE; DATE THE BACK OF EACH PICTURE

FASTEN PICTURES OF CHILDREN'S DEPARTURE APPEARANCE; DATE THE BACK OF EACH PICTURE

INSTRUCTIONS PROVIDED TO OTHER PARTY REGARDING CHILDREN

MONTH OF:				
DATE	CHILD'S NAME	SICKNESS/INJURY	ITEMS SENT	INSTRUCTIONS PROVIDED

DETAILS:

DETAILS:

DETAILS:

DETAILS:

INSTRUCTIONS PROVIDED TO OTHER PARTY REGARDING CHILDREN

MONTH OF:				
DATE	CHILD'S NAME	SICKNESS/INJURY	ITEMS SENT	INSTRUCTIONS PROVIDED

DETAILS:

DETAILS:

DETAILS:

DETAILS:

INSTRUCTIONS PROVIDED TO OTHER PARTY REGARDING CHILDREN

MONTH OF:				
DATE	CHILD'S NAME	SICKNESS/INJURY	ITEMS SENT	INSTRUCTIONS PROVIDED
DETAILS:				
DETAILS:				
DETAILS:				
DETAILS:				

INSTRUCTIONS PROVIDED TO OTHER PARTY REGARDING CHILDREN

MONTH OF:				
DATE	CHILD'S NAME	SICKNESS/INJURY	ITEMS SENT	INSTRUCTIONS PROVIDED

DETAILS:

DETAILS:

DETAILS:

DETAILS:

CHILDREN'S RETURN

MONTH OF:					
DATE	WHO	LATE OR NO SHOW	ISSUES DURING DROP OFF	PROPER CAR SEATS?	CHILDREN'S REACTION TO LEAVING OTHER PARTY
DETAILS:					
DETAILS:					
DETAILS:					
DETAILS:					
DETAILS:					

CHILDREN'S RETURN

MONTH OF:					
DATE	WHO	LATE OR NO SHOW	ISSUES DURING DROP OFF	PROPER CAR SEATS?	CHILDREN'S REACTION TO LEAVING OTHER PARTY
DETAILS:					
DETAILS:					
DETAILS:					
DETAILS:					
DETAILS:					

CHILDREN'S RETURN

MONTH OF:					
DATE	WHO	LATE OR NO SHOW	ISSUES DURING DROP OFF	PROPER CAR SEATS?	CHILDREN'S REACTION TO LEAVING OTHER PARTY

DETAILS:

DATE	WHO	LATE OR NO SHOW	ISSUES DURING DROP OFF	PROPER CAR SEATS?	CHILDREN'S REACTION TO LEAVING OTHER PARTY

DETAILS:

DATE	WHO	LATE OR NO SHOW	ISSUES DURING DROP OFF	PROPER CAR SEATS?	CHILDREN'S REACTION TO LEAVING OTHER PARTY

DETAILS:

DATE	WHO	LATE OR NO SHOW	ISSUES DURING DROP OFF	PROPER CAR SEATS?	CHILDREN'S REACTION TO LEAVING OTHER PARTY

DETAILS:

DATE	WHO	LATE OR NO SHOW	ISSUES DURING DROP OFF	PROPER CAR SEATS?	CHILDREN'S REACTION TO LEAVING OTHER PARTY

DETAILS:

FASTEN PICTURES OF CHILDREN'S RETURN APPEARANCE; DATE THE BACK OF EACH PICTURE

FASTEN PICTURES OF CHILDREN'S RETURN
APPEARANCE; DATE THE BACK OF EACH PICTURE

FASTEN PICTURES OF CHILDREN'S RETURN APPEARANCE; DATE THE BACK OF EACH PICTURE

VISIT DETAILS

MONTH OF:					
DATE	CHILD'S NAME	ILLNESS OR INJURIES	ITEMS NOT RETURNED OR BROKEN	PROPER FITTING CLEAN CLOTHING	BROKEN PROMISES OR MISSED CELEBRATIONS

DETAILS:

DETAILS:

DETAILS:

DETAILS:

VISIT DETAILS

MONTH OF:					
DATE	CHILD'S NAME	ILLNESS OR INJURIES	ITEMS NOT RETURNED OR BROKEN	PROPER FITTING CLEAN CLOTHING	BROKEN PROMISES OR MISSED CELEBRATIONS
DETAILS:					
DETAILS:					
DETAILS:					
DETAILS:					

VISIT DETAILS

MONTH OF:					
DATE	**CHILD'S NAME**	**ILLNESS OR INJURIES**	**ITEMS NOT RETURNED OR BROKEN**	**PROPER FITTING CLEAN CLOTHING**	**BROKEN PROMISES OR MISSED CELEBRATIONS**
DETAILS:					
DETAILS:					
DETAILS:					
DETAILS:					

VISIT DETAILS

MONTH OF:					
DATE	CHILD'S NAME	ILLNESS OR INJURIES	ITEMS NOT RETURNED OR BROKEN	PROPER FITTING CLEAN CLOTHING	BROKEN PROMISES OR MISSED CELEBRATIONS

DETAILS:

DETAILS:

DETAILS:

DETAILS:

CHILDREN'S MONTHLY ACCOMPLISHMENTS

DATE	CHILD'S NAME	ACCOMPLISHMENT TYPE (ACADEMIC, SOCIAL, EXTRA-CURRICULER...)	CLUB, AWARD TITLE	ADVISE OTHER PARENT? IF YES, WHAT METHOD?	DID PARENT ATTEND OR CALL CHILD?

(Insert Date)

Re: (Other Parent's Name)

(Insert Your Name)
(Insert Street Address)
(Insert Street Address)
(Insert Phone Number)

(Insert Requesting Agency)
Central Records Division
(Insert Agency's Street Address)
(Insert Agency's Street Address)

To (Insert Agency Name) Central Records:

We are writing to request all offense records on (insert name including DOB) from (recommend 6 month increments) Please also include all assistance calls for address:

(Insert other parent's address here)

We can be reached at (insert your phone number). We appreciate your time and quick response.

Sincerely,

(Your signature)

(Your Name)

PERIODIC PUBLIC RECORD REQUEST

DATE	REPORTING AGENCY (911, POLICE REPORTS, CLERK OF COURTS)	TYPE OF REPORT (CIVIL, DOMESTIC, CRIMINAL)	PERSONS INVOLVED	ANY CRIMINAL CHARGES FILED	REPORT DETAILS

ATTACH REPORTS HERE

ATTACH REPORTS HERE

ADDITIONAL NOTES PAGE FOR MONTH:

ADDITIONAL NOTES PAGE FOR MONTH:

ADDITIONAL NOTES PAGE FOR MONTH:

MONTH 2

PHONE LOG FOR MONTH:

DATE	CALL LENGTH	CALL TYPE	WHO CALLED	CONVERSATION DETAILS/CHILDREN'S REACTION

PHONE LOG FOR MONTH:

DATE	CALL LENGTH	CALL TYPE	WHO CALLED	CONVERSATION DETAILS/CHILDREN'S REACTION

PHONE LOG FOR MONTH:

DATE	CALL LENGTH	CALL TYPE	WHO CALLED	CONVERSATION DETAILS/CHILDREN'S REACTION

PHONE LOG FOR MONTH:

DATE	CALL LENGTH	CALL TYPE	WHO CALLED	CONVERSATION DETAILS/CHILDREN'S REACTION

PHONE LOG FOR MONTH:

DATE	CALL LENGTH	CALL TYPE	WHO CALLED	CONVERSATION DETAILS/CHILDREN'S REACTION

ATTACH PICTURES OF SIGNIFICANT TEXT MESSAGES

ATTACH PICTURES OF SIGNIFICANT TEXT MESSAGES

ATTACH PICTURES OF SIGNIFICANT TEXT MESSAGES

CHILDREN'S PICK UP

MONTH OF:					
DATE	WHO	LATE OR NO SHOW	PICK UP ISSUES	PROPER CAR SEATS?	CHILDREN'S REACTION TO INITIATION OF VISIT

DETAILS:

DETAILS:

DETAILS:

DETAILS:

DETAILS:

CHILDREN'S PICK UP

MONTH OF:					
DATE	WHO	LATE OR NO SHOW	PICK UP ISSUES	PROPER CAR SEATS?	CHILDREN'S REACTION TO INITIATION OF VISIT

DETAILS:

DETAILS:

DETAILS:

DETAILS:

DETAILS:

CHILDREN'S PICK UP

MONTH OF:					
DATE	WHO	LATE OR NO SHOW	PICK UP ISSUES	PROPER CAR SEATS?	CHILDREN'S REACTION TO INITIATION OF VISIT
DETAILS:					
DETAILS:					
DETAILS:					
DETAILS:					
DETAILS:					

FASTEN PICTURES OF CHILDREN'S DEPARTURE
APPEARANCE; DATE THE BACK OF EACH PICTURE

FASTEN PICTURES OF CHILDREN'S DEPARTURE APPEARANCE; DATE THE BACK OF EACH PICTURE

FASTEN PICTURES OF CHILDREN'S DEPARTURE APPEARANCE; DATE THE BACK OF EACH PICTURE

INSTRUCTIONS PROVIDED TO OTHER PARTY
REGARDING CHILDREN

MONTH OF:				
DATE	CHILD'S NAME	SICKNESS/INJURY	ITEMS SENT	INSTRUCTIONS PROVIDED
DETAILS:				
DETAILS:				
DETAILS:				
DETAILS:				

INSTRUCTIONS PROVIDED TO OTHER PARTY REGARDING CHILDREN

MONTH OF:				
DATE	CHILD'S NAME	SICKNESS/INJURY	ITEMS SENT	INSTRUCTIONS PROVIDED
DETAILS:				
DETAILS:				
DETAILS:				
DETAILS:				

INSTRUCTIONS PROVIDED TO OTHER PARTY REGARDING CHILDREN

MONTH OF:				
DATE	**CHILD'S NAME**	**SICKNESS/INJURY**	**ITEMS SENT**	**INSTRUCTIONS PROVIDED**
DETAILS:				
DETAILS:				
DETAILS:				
DETAILS:				

INSTRUCTIONS PROVIDED TO OTHER PARTY REGARDING CHILDREN

MONTH OF:				
DATE	CHILD'S NAME	SICKNESS/INJURY	ITEMS SENT	INSTRUCTIONS PROVIDED

DETAILS:

DETAILS:

DETAILS:

DETAILS:

CHILDREN'S RETURN

MONTH OF:					
DATE	WHO	LATE OR NO SHOW	ISSUES DURING DROP OFF	PROPER CAR SEATS?	CHILDREN'S REACTION TO LEAVING OTHER PARTY

DETAILS:

DETAILS:

DETAILS:

DETAILS:

DETAILS:

CHILDREN'S RETURN

MONTH OF:					
DATE	WHO	LATE OR NO SHOW	ISSUES DURING DROP OFF	PROPER CAR SEATS?	CHILDREN'S REACTION TO LEAVING OTHER PARTY
DETAILS:					
DETAILS:					
DETAILS:					
DETAILS:					
DETAILS:					

CHILDREN'S RETURN

MONTH OF:					
DATE	WHO	LATE OR NO SHOW	ISSUES DURING DROP OFF	PROPER CAR SEATS?	CHILDREN'S REACTION TO LEAVING OTHER PARTY

DETAILS:

DETAILS:

DETAILS:

DETAILS:

DETAILS:

FASTEN PICTURES OF CHILDREN'S RETURN APPEARANCE; DATE THE BACK OF EACH PICTURE

FASTEN PICTURES OF CHILDREN'S RETURN APPEARANCE; DATE THE BACK OF EACH PICTURE

FASTEN PICTURES OF CHILDREN'S RETURN APPEARANCE; DATE THE BACK OF EACH PICTURE

VISIT DETAILS

MONTH OF:					
DATE	CHILD'S NAME	ILLNESS OR INJURIES	ITEMS NOT RETURNED OR BROKEN	PROPER FITTING CLEAN CLOTHING	BROKEN PROMISES OR MISSED CELEBRATIONS

DETAILS:

DETAILS:

DETAILS:

DETAILS:

VISIT DETAILS

MONTH OF:					
DATE	CHILD'S NAME	ILLNESS OR INJURIES	ITEMS NOT RETURNED OR BROKEN	PROPER FITTING CLEAN CLOTHING	BROKEN PROMISES OR MISSED CELEBRATIONS
DETAILS:					
DETAILS:					
DETAILS:					
DETAILS:					

VISIT DETAILS

MONTH OF:					
DATE	CHILD'S NAME	ILLNESS OR INJURIES	ITEMS NOT RETURNED OR BROKEN	PROPER FITTING CLEAN CLOTHING	BROKEN PROMISES OR MISSED CELEBRATIONS

DETAILS:

DETAILS:

DETAILS:

DETAILS:

VISIT DETAILS

MONTH OF:					
DATE	CHILD'S NAME	ILLNESS OR INJURIES	ITEMS NOT RETURNED OR BROKEN	PROPER FITTING CLEAN CLOTHING	BROKEN PROMISES OR MISSED CELEBRATIONS

DETAILS:

DETAILS:

DETAILS:

DETAILS:

CHILDREN'S MONTHLY ACCOMPLISHMENTS

DATE	CHILD'S NAME	ACCOMPLISHMENT TYPE (ACADEMIC, SOCIAL, EXTRA-CURRICULER...)	CLUB, AWARD TITLE	ADVISE OTHER PARENT? IF YES, WHAT METHOD?	DID PARENT ATTEND OR CALL CHILD?

ADDITIONAL NOTES PAGE FOR MONTH:

ADDITIONAL NOTES PAGE FOR MONTH:

ADDITIONAL NOTES PAGE FOR MONTH:

_____
_____
_____
_____
_____
_____
_____
_____
_____
_____
_____
_____
_____
_____
_____
_____
_____
_____
_____
_____
_____
_____
_____
_____

MONTH 3

PHONE LOG FOR MONTH:

DATE	CALL LENGTH	CALL TYPE	WHO CALLED	CONVERSATION DETAILS/CHILDREN'S REACTION

PHONE LOG FOR MONTH:

DATE	CALL LENGTH	CALL TYPE	WHO CALLED	CONVERSATION DETAILS/CHILDREN'S REACTION

PHONE LOG FOR MONTH:

DATE	CALL LENGTH	CALL TYPE	WHO CALLED	CONVERSATION DETAILS/CHILDREN'S REACTION

PHONE LOG FOR MONTH:

DATE	CALL LENGTH	CALL TYPE	WHO CALLED	CONVERSATION DETAILS/CHILDREN'S REACTION

ATTACH PICTURES OF SIGNIFICANT TEXT MESSAGES

ATTACH PICTURES OF SIGNIFICANT TEXT MESSAGES

ATTACH PICTURES OF SIGNIFICANT TEXT MESSAGES

CHILDREN'S PICK UP

MONTH OF:					
DATE	WHO	LATE OR NO SHOW	PICK UP ISSUES	PROPER CAR SEATS?	CHILDREN'S REACTION TO INITIATION OF VISIT
DETAILS:					
DETAILS:					
DETAILS:					
DETAILS:					
DETAILS:					

CHILDREN'S PICK UP

MONTH OF:					
DATE	WHO	LATE OR NO SHOW	PICK UP ISSUES	PROPER CAR SEATS?	CHILDREN'S REACTION TO INITIATION OF VISIT
DETAILS:					
DETAILS:					
DETAILS:					
DETAILS:					
DETAILS:					

CHILDREN'S PICK UP

MONTH OF:					
DATE	WHO	LATE OR NO SHOW	PICK UP ISSUES	PROPER CAR SEATS?	CHILDREN'S REACTION TO INITIATION OF VISIT

DETAILS:

DETAILS:

DETAILS:

DETAILS:

DETAILS:

FASTEN PICTURES OF CHILDREN'S DEPARTURE APPEARANCE; DATE THE BACK OF EACH PICTURE

FASTEN PICTURES OF CHILDREN'S DEPARTURE APPEARANCE; DATE THE BACK OF EACH PICTURE

FASTEN PICTURES OF CHILDREN'S DEPARTURE APPEARANCE; DATE THE BACK OF EACH PICTURE

INSTRUCTIONS PROVIDED TO OTHER PARTY REGARDING CHILDREN

MONTH OF:				
DATE	CHILD'S NAME	SICKNESS/INJURY	ITEMS SENT	INSTRUCTIONS PROVIDED
DETAILS:				
DETAILS:				
DETAILS:				
DETAILS:				

INSTRUCTIONS PROVIDED TO OTHER PARTY REGARDING CHILDREN

MONTH OF:				
DATE	CHILD'S NAME	SICKNESS/INJURY	ITEMS SENT	INSTRUCTIONS PROVIDED
DETAILS:				
DETAILS:				
DETAILS:				
DETAILS:				

INSTRUCTIONS PROVIDED TO OTHER PARTY REGARDING CHILDREN

MONTH OF:				
DATE	CHILD'S NAME	SICKNESS/INJURY	ITEMS SENT	INSTRUCTIONS PROVIDED

DETAILS:

DETAILS:

DETAILS:

DETAILS:

INSTRUCTIONS PROVIDED TO OTHER PARTY REGARDING CHILDREN

MONTH OF:				
DATE	**CHILD'S NAME**	**SICKNESS/INJURY**	**ITEMS SENT**	**INSTRUCTIONS PROVIDED**
DETAILS:				
DETAILS:				
DETAILS:				
DETAILS:				

CHILDREN'S RETURN

MONTH OF:					
DATE	WHO	LATE OR NO SHOW	ISSUES DURING DROP OFF	PROPER CAR SEATS?	CHILDREN'S REACTION TO LEAVING OTHER PARTY
DETAILS:					
DETAILS:					
DETAILS:					
DETAILS:					
DETAILS:					

CHILDREN'S RETURN

MONTH OF:					
DATE	WHO	LATE OR NO SHOW	ISSUES DURING DROP OFF	PROPER CAR SEATS?	CHILDREN'S REACTION TO LEAVING OTHER PARTY
DETAILS:					
DETAILS:					
DETAILS:					
DETAILS:					
DETAILS:					

CHILDREN'S RETURN

MONTH OF:					
DATE	WHO	LATE OR NO SHOW	ISSUES DURING DROP OFF	PROPER CAR SEATS?	CHILDREN'S REACTION TO LEAVING OTHER PARTY
DETAILS:					
DETAILS:					
DETAILS:					
DETAILS:					
DETAILS:					

FASTEN PICTURES OF CHILDREN'S RETURN APPEARANCE; DATE THE BACK OF EACH PICTURE

FASTEN PICTURES OF CHILDREN'S RETURN APPEARANCE; DATE THE BACK OF EACH PICTURE

FASTEN PICTURES OF CHILDREN'S RETURN APPEARANCE; DATE THE BACK OF EACH PICTURE

VISIT DETAILS

MONTH OF:					
DATE	CHILD'S NAME	ILLNESS OR INJURIES	ITEMS NOT RETURNED OR BROKEN	PROPER FITTING CLEAN CLOTHING	BROKEN PROMISES OR MISSED CELEBRATIONS

DETAILS:

DETAILS:

DETAILS:

DETAILS:

VISIT DETAILS

MONTH OF:					
DATE	CHILD'S NAME	ILLNESS OR INJURIES	ITEMS NOT RETURNED OR BROKEN	PROPER FITTING CLEAN CLOTHING	BROKEN PROMISES OR MISSED CELEBRATIONS

DETAILS:

DETAILS:

DETAILS:

DETAILS:

VISIT DETAILS

MONTH OF:					
DATE	CHILD'S NAME	ILLNESS OR INJURIES	ITEMS NOT RETURNED OR BROKEN	PROPER FITTING CLEAN CLOTHING	BROKEN PROMISES OR MISSED CELEBRATIONS
DETAILS:					
DETAILS:					
DETAILS:					
DETAILS:					

VISIT DETAILS

MONTH OF:					
DATE	CHILD'S NAME	ILLNESS OR INJURIES	ITEMS NOT RETURNED OR BROKEN	PROPER FITTING CLEAN CLOTHING	BROKEN PROMISES OR MISSED CELEBRATIONS

DETAILS:

DETAILS:

DETAILS:

DETAILS:

CHILDREN'S MONTHLY ACCOMPLISHMENTS

DATE	CHILD'S NAME	ACCOMPLISHMENT TYPE (ACADEMIC, SOCIAL, EXTRA-CURRICULER...)	CLUB, AWARD TITLE	ADVISE OTHER PARENT? IF YES, WHAT METHOD?	DID PARENT ATTEND OR CALL CHILD?

ADDITIONAL NOTES PAGE FOR MONTH:

ADDITIONAL NOTES PAGE FOR MONTH:

_____

_____

_____

_____

_____

_____

_____

_____

_____

_____

_____

_____

_____

_____

_____

_____

_____

_____

_____

_____

_____

_____

ADDITIONAL NOTES PAGE FOR MONTH:

_____
_____
_____
_____
_____
_____
_____
_____
_____
_____
_____
_____
_____
_____
_____
_____
_____
_____
_____
_____
_____
_____

MONTH 4

PHONE LOG FOR MONTH:

DATE	CALL LENGTH	CALL TYPE	WHO CALLED	CONVERSATION DETAILS/CHILDREN'S REACTION

PHONE LOG FOR MONTH:

DATE	CALL LENGTH	CALL TYPE	WHO CALLED	CONVERSATION DETAILS/CHILDREN'S REACTION

PHONE LOG FOR MONTH:

DATE	CALL LENGTH	CALL TYPE	WHO CALLED	CONVERSATION DETAILS/CHILDREN'S REACTION

PHONE LOG FOR MONTH:

DATE	CALL LENGTH	CALL TYPE	WHO CALLED	CONVERSATION DETAILS/CHILDREN'S REACTION

ATTACH PICTURES OF SIGNIFICANT TEXT MESSAGES

ATTACH PICTURES OF SIGNIFICANT TEXT MESSAGES

ATTACH PICTURES OF SIGNIFICANT TEXT MESSAGES

CHILDREN'S PICK UP

MONTH OF:					
DATE	WHO	LATE OR NO SHOW	PICK UP ISSUES	PROPER CAR SEATS?	CHILDREN'S REACTION TO INITIATION OF VISIT

DETAILS:

DETAILS:

DETAILS:

DETAILS:

DETAILS:

CHILDREN'S PICK UP

MONTH OF:					
DATE	WHO	LATE OR NO SHOW	PICK UP ISSUES	PROPER CAR SEATS?	CHILDREN'S REACTION TO INITIATION OF VISIT
DETAILS:					
DETAILS:					
DETAILS:					
DETAILS:					
DETAILS:					

CHILDREN'S PICK UP

MONTH OF:					
DATE	WHO	LATE OR NO SHOW	PICK UP ISSUES	PROPER CAR SEATS?	CHILDREN'S REACTION TO INITIATION OF VISIT

DETAILS:

DETAILS:

DETAILS:

DETAILS:

DETAILS:

FASTEN PICTURES OF CHILDREN'S DEPARTURE APPEARANCE; DATE THE BACK OF EACH PICTURE

FASTEN PICTURES OF CHILDREN'S DEPARTURE APPEARANCE; DATE THE BACK OF EACH PICTURE

FASTEN PICTURES OF CHILDREN'S DEPARTURE APPEARANCE; DATE THE BACK OF EACH PICTURE

INSTRUCTIONS PROVIDED TO OTHER PARTY REGARDING CHILDREN

MONTH OF:				
DATE	CHILD'S NAME	SICKNESS/INJURY	ITEMS SENT	INSTRUCTIONS PROVIDED

DETAILS:

DETAILS:

DETAILS:

DETAILS:

INSTRUCTIONS PROVIDED TO OTHER PARTY REGARDING CHILDREN

MONTH OF:				
DATE	CHILD'S NAME	SICKNESS/INJURY	ITEMS SENT	INSTRUCTIONS PROVIDED
DETAILS:				
DETAILS:				
DETAILS:				
DETAILS:				

INSTRUCTIONS PROVIDED TO OTHER PARTY REGARDING CHILDREN

MONTH OF:				
DATE	CHILD'S NAME	SICKNESS/INJURY	ITEMS SENT	INSTRUCTIONS PROVIDED

DETAILS:

DETAILS:

DETAILS:

DETAILS:

INSTRUCTIONS PROVIDED TO OTHER PARTY REGARDING CHILDREN

MONTH OF:				
DATE	CHILD'S NAME	SICKNESS/INJURY	ITEMS SENT	INSTRUCTIONS PROVIDED
DETAILS:				
DETAILS:				
DETAILS:				
DETAILS:				

CHILDREN'S RETURN

MONTH OF:					
DATE	WHO	LATE OR NO SHOW	ISSUES DURING DROP OFF	PROPER CAR SEATS?	CHILDREN'S REACTION TO LEAVING OTHER PARTY

DETAILS:

DETAILS:

DETAILS:

DETAILS:

DETAILS:

CHILDREN'S RETURN

MONTH OF:					
DATE	WHO	LATE OR NO SHOW	ISSUES DURING DROP OFF	PROPER CAR SEATS?	CHILDREN'S REACTION TO LEAVING OTHER PARTY
DETAILS:					
DETAILS:					
DETAILS:					
DETAILS:					
DETAILS:					

CHILDREN'S RETURN

MONTH OF:					
DATE	WHO	LATE OR NO SHOW	ISSUES DURING DROP OFF	PROPER CAR SEATS?	CHILDREN'S REACTION TO LEAVING OTHER PARTY

DETAILS:

DETAILS:

DETAILS:

DETAILS:

DETAILS:

FASTEN PICTURES OF CHILDREN'S RETURN APPEARANCE; DATE THE BACK OF EACH PICTURE

FASTEN PICTURES OF CHILDREN'S RETURN APPEARANCE; DATE THE BACK OF EACH PICTURE

FASTEN PICTURES OF CHILDREN'S RETURN APPEARANCE; DATE THE BACK OF EACH PICTURE

VISIT DETAILS

MONTH OF:					
DATE	CHILD'S NAME	ILLNESS OR INJURIES	ITEMS NOT RETURNED OR BROKEN	PROPER FITTING CLEAN CLOTHING	BROKEN PROMISES OR MISSED CELEBRATIONS
DETAILS:					
DETAILS:					
DETAILS:					
DETAILS:					

VISIT DETAILS

MONTH OF:					
DATE	CHILD'S NAME	ILLNESS OR INJURIES	ITEMS NOT RETURNED OR BROKEN	PROPER FITTING CLEAN CLOTHING	BROKEN PROMISES OR MISSED CELEBRATIONS

DETAILS:

DETAILS:

DETAILS:

DETAILS:

VISIT DETAILS

MONTH OF:					
DATE	CHILD'S NAME	ILLNESS OR INJURIES	ITEMS NOT RETURNED OR BROKEN	PROPER FITTING CLEAN CLOTHING	BROKEN PROMISES OR MISSED CELEBRATIONS
DETAILS:					
DETAILS:					
DETAILS:					
DETAILS:					

VISIT DETAILS

MONTH OF:					
DATE	CHILD'S NAME	ILLNESS OR INJURIES	ITEMS NOT RETURNED OR BROKEN	PROPER FITTING CLEAN CLOTHING	BROKEN PROMISES OR MISSED CELEBRATIONS

DETAILS:

DETAILS:

DETAILS:

DETAILS:

CHILDREN'S MONTHLY ACCOMPLISHMENTS

DATE	CHILD'S NAME	ACCOMPLISHMENT TYPE (ACADEMIC, SOCIAL, EXTRA-CURRICULER...)	CLUB, AWARD TITLE	ADVISE OTHER PARENT? IF YES, WHAT METHOD?	DID PARENT ATTEND OR CALL CHILD?

ADDITIONAL NOTES PAGE FOR MONTH:

_____

_____

_____

_____

_____

_____

_____

_____

_____

_____

_____

_____

_____

_____

_____

_____

_____

_____

_____

_____

_____

_____

ADDITIONAL NOTES PAGE FOR MONTH:

ADDITIONAL NOTES PAGE FOR MONTH:

_____

_____

_____

_____

_____

_____

_____

_____

_____

_____

_____

_____

_____

_____

_____

_____

_____

_____

_____

_____

MONTH 5

PHONE LOG FOR MONTH:

DATE	CALL LENGTH	CALL TYPE	WHO CALLED	CONVERSATION DETAILS/CHILDREN'S REACTION

PHONE LOG FOR MONTH:

DATE	CALL LENGTH	CALL TYPE	WHO CALLED	CONVERSATION DETAILS/CHILDREN'S REACTION

PHONE LOG FOR MONTH:

DATE	CALL LENGTH	CALL TYPE	WHO CALLED	CONVERSATION DETAILS/CHILDREN'S REACTION

PHONE LOG FOR MONTH:

DATE	CALL LENGTH	CALL TYPE	WHO CALLED	CONVERSATION DETAILS/CHILDREN'S REACTION

ATTACH PICTURES OF SIGNIFICANT TEXT MESSAGES

ATTACH PICTURES OF SIGNIFICANT TEXT MESSAGES

ATTACH PICTURES OF SIGNIFICANT TEXT MESSAGES

CHILDREN'S PICK UP

MONTH OF:					
DATE	**WHO**	**LATE OR NO SHOW**	**PICK UP ISSUES**	**PROPER CAR SEATS?**	**CHILDREN'S REACTION TO INITIATION OF VISIT**
DETAILS:					
DETAILS:					
DETAILS:					
DETAILS:					
DETAILS:					

CHILDREN'S PICK UP

MONTH OF:					
DATE	WHO	LATE OR NO SHOW	PICK UP ISSUES	PROPER CAR SEATS?	CHILDREN'S REACTION TO INITIATION OF VISIT
DETAILS:					
DETAILS:					
DETAILS:					
DETAILS:					
DETAILS:					

CHILDREN'S PICK UP

MONTH OF:					
DATE	WHO	LATE OR NO SHOW	PICK UP ISSUES	PROPER CAR SEATS?	CHILDREN'S REACTION TO INITIATION OF VISIT
DETAILS:					
DETAILS:					
DETAILS:					
DETAILS:					
DETAILS:					

FASTEN PICTURES OF CHILDREN'S DEPARTURE APPEARANCE; DATE THE BACK OF EACH PICTURE

FASTEN PICTURES OF CHILDREN'S DEPARTURE APPEARANCE; DATE THE BACK OF EACH PICTURE

FASTEN PICTURES OF CHILDREN'S DEPARTURE APPEARANCE; DATE THE BACK OF EACH PICTURE

INSTRUCTIONS PROVIDED TO OTHER PARTY REGARDING CHILDREN

MONTH OF:				
DATE	CHILD'S NAME	SICKNESS/INJURY	ITEMS SENT	INSTRUCTIONS PROVIDED
DETAILS:				
DETAILS:				
DETAILS:				
DETAILS:				

INSTRUCTIONS PROVIDED TO OTHER PARTY
REGARDING CHILDREN

MONTH OF:				
DATE	CHILD'S NAME	SICKNESS/INJURY	ITEMS SENT	INSTRUCTIONS PROVIDED
DETAILS:				
DETAILS:				
DETAILS:				
DETAILS:				

INSTRUCTIONS PROVIDED TO OTHER PARTY REGARDING CHILDREN

MONTH OF:				
DATE	CHILD'S NAME	SICKNESS/INJURY	ITEMS SENT	INSTRUCTIONS PROVIDED

DETAILS:

DATE	CHILD'S NAME	SICKNESS/INJURY	ITEMS SENT	INSTRUCTIONS PROVIDED

DETAILS:

DATE	CHILD'S NAME	SICKNESS/INJURY	ITEMS SENT	INSTRUCTIONS PROVIDED

DETAILS:

DATE	CHILD'S NAME	SICKNESS/INJURY	ITEMS SENT	INSTRUCTIONS PROVIDED

DETAILS:

INSTRUCTIONS PROVIDED TO OTHER PARTY REGARDING CHILDREN

MONTH OF:				
DATE	**CHILD'S NAME**	**SICKNESS/INJURY**	**ITEMS SENT**	**INSTRUCTIONS PROVIDED**

DETAILS:

DETAILS:

DETAILS:

DETAILS:

CHILDREN'S RETURN

MONTH OF:					
DATE	WHO	LATE OR NO SHOW	ISSUES DURING DROP OFF	PROPER CAR SEATS?	CHILDREN'S REACTION TO LEAVING OTHER PARTY

DETAILS:

DETAILS:

DETAILS:

DETAILS:

DETAILS:

CHILDREN'S RETURN

MONTH OF:					
DATE	WHO	LATE OR NO SHOW	ISSUES DURING DROP OFF	PROPER CAR SEATS?	CHILDREN'S REACTION TO LEAVING OTHER PARTY

DETAILS:

DETAILS:

DETAILS:

DETAILS:

DETAILS:

CHILDREN'S RETURN

MONTH OF:					
DATE	WHO	LATE OR NO SHOW	ISSUES DURING DROP OFF	PROPER CAR SEATS?	CHILDREN'S REACTION TO LEAVING OTHER PARTY
DETAILS:					
DETAILS:					
DETAILS:					
DETAILS:					
DETAILS:					

FASTEN PICTURES OF CHILDREN'S RETURN APPEARANCE; DATE THE BACK OF EACH PICTURE

FASTEN PICTURES OF CHILDREN'S RETURN APPEARANCE; DATE THE BACK OF EACH PICTURE

FASTEN PICTURES OF CHILDREN'S RETURN APPEARANCE; DATE THE BACK OF EACH PICTURE

VISIT DETAILS

MONTH OF					
DATE	CHILD'S NAME	ILLNESS OR INJURIES	ITEMS NOT RETURNED OR BROKEN	PROPER FITTING CLEAN CLOTHING	BROKEN PROMISES OR MISSED CELEBRATIONS
DETAILS:					
DETAILS:					
DETAILS:					
DETAILS:					

VISIT DETAILS

MONTH OF:					
DATE	CHILD'S NAME	ILLNESS OR INJURIES	ITEMS NOT RETURNED OR BROKEN	PROPER FITTING CLEAN CLOTHING	BROKEN PROMISES OR MISSED CELEBRATIONS

DETAILS:

DETAILS:

DETAILS:

DETAILS:

VISIT DETAILS

MONTH OF:					
DATE	CHILD'S NAME	ILLNESS OR INJURIES	ITEMS NOT RETURNED OR BROKEN	PROPER FITTING CLEAN CLOTHING	BROKEN PROMISES OR MISSED CELEBRATIONS
DETAILS:					
DETAILS:					
DETAILS:					
DETAILS:					

VISIT DETAILS

MONTH OF:					
DATE	CHILD'S NAME	ILLNESS OR INJURIES	ITEMS NOT RETURNED OR BROKEN	PROPER FITTING CLEAN CLOTHING	BROKEN PROMISES OR MISSED CELEBRATIONS
DETAILS:					
DETAILS:					
DETAILS:					
DETAILS:					

CHILDREN'S MONTHLY ACCOMPLISHMENTS

DATE	CHILD'S NAME	ACCOMPLISHMENT TYPE (ACADEMIC, SOCIAL, EXTRA-CURRICULER...)	CLUB, AWARD TITLE	ADVISE OTHER PARENT? IF YES, WHAT METHOD?	DID PARENT ATTEND OR CALL CHILD?

ADDITIONAL NOTES PAGE FOR MONTH:

_____

_____

_____

_____

_____

_____

_____

_____

_____

_____

_____

_____

_____

_____

_____

_____

_____

_____

_____

_____

_____

_____

_____

ADDITIONAL NOTES PAGE FOR MONTH:

_____

_____

_____

_____

_____

_____

_____

_____

_____

_____

_____

_____

_____

_____

_____

_____

_____

_____

_____

_____

_____

_____

ADDITIONAL NOTES PAGE FOR MONTH:

MONTH 6

PHONE LOG FOR MONTH:

DATE	CALL LENGTH	CALL TYPE	WHO CALLED	CONVERSATION DETAILS/CHILDREN'S REACTION

PHONE LOG FOR MONTH:

DATE	CALL LENGTH	CALL TYPE	WHO CALLED	CONVERSATION DETAILS/CHILDREN'S REACTION

PHONE LOG FOR MONTH:

DATE	CALL LENGTH	CALL TYPE	WHO CALLED	CONVERSATION DETAILS/CHILDREN'S REACTION

PHONE LOG FOR MONTH:

DATE	CALL LENGTH	CALL TYPE	WHO CALLED	CONVERSATION DETAILS/CHILDREN'S REACTION

ATTACH PICTURES OF SIGNIFICANT TEXT MESSAGES

ATTACH PICTURES OF SIGNIFICANT TEXT MESSAGES

ATTACH PICTURES OF SIGNIFICANT TEXT MESSAGES

CHILDREN'S PICK UP

MONTH OF:					
DATE	**WHO**	**LATE OR NO SHOW**	**PICK UP ISSUES**	**PROPER CAR SEATS?**	**CHILDREN'S REACTION TO INITIATION OF VISIT**
DETAILS:					
DETAILS:					
DETAILS:					
DETAILS:					
DETAILS:					

CHILDREN'S PICK UP

MONTH OF:					
DATE	WHO	LATE OR NO SHOW	PICK UP ISSUES	PROPER CAR SEATS?	CHILDREN'S REACTION TO INITIATION OF VISIT

DETAILS:

DETAILS:

DETAILS:

DETAILS:

DETAILS:

CHILDREN'S PICK UP

MONTH OF:					
DATE	WHO	LATE OR NO SHOW	PICK UP ISSUES	PROPER CAR SEATS?	CHILDREN'S REACTION TO INITIATION OF VISIT
DETAILS:					
DETAILS:					
DETAILS:					
DETAILS:					
DETAILS:					

FASTEN PICTURES OF CHILDREN'S DEPARTURE APPEARANCE; DATE THE BACK OF EACH PICTURE

FASTEN PICTURES OF CHILDREN'S DEPARTURE APPEARANCE; DATE THE BACK OF EACH PICTURE

FASTEN PICTURES OF CHILDREN'S DEPARTURE APPEARANCE; DATE THE BACK OF EACH PICTURE

INSTRUCTIONS PROVIDED TO OTHER PARTY REGARDING CHILDREN

MONTH OF:				
DATE	**CHILD'S NAME**	**SICKNESS/INJURY**	**ITEMS SENT**	**INSTRUCTIONS PROVIDED**
DETAILS:				
DETAILS:				
DETAILS:				
DETAILS:				

INSTRUCTIONS PROVIDED TO OTHER PARTY REGARDING CHILDREN

DATE	CHILD'S NAME	SICKNESS/INJURY	ITEMS SENT	INSTRUCTIONS PROVIDED
MONTH OF:				

DETAILS:

DATE	CHILD'S NAME	SICKNESS/INJURY	ITEMS SENT	INSTRUCTIONS PROVIDED

DETAILS:

DATE	CHILD'S NAME	SICKNESS/INJURY	ITEMS SENT	INSTRUCTIONS PROVIDED

DETAILS:

DATE	CHILD'S NAME	SICKNESS/INJURY	ITEMS SENT	INSTRUCTIONS PROVIDED

DETAILS:

INSTRUCTIONS PROVIDED TO OTHER PARTY REGARDING CHILDREN

MONTH OF:				
DATE	CHILD'S NAME	SICKNESS/INJURY	ITEMS SENT	INSTRUCTIONS PROVIDED
DETAILS:				
DETAILS:				
DETAILS:				
DETAILS:				

INSTRUCTIONS PROVIDED TO OTHER PARTY REGARDING CHILDREN

MONTH OF:				
DATE	CHILD'S NAME	SICKNESS/INJURY	ITEMS SENT	INSTRUCTIONS PROVIDED
DETAILS:				
DETAILS:				
DETAILS:				
DETAILS:				

CHILDREN'S RETURN

MONTH OF:					
DATE	WHO	LATE OR NO SHOW	ISSUES DURING DROP OFF	PROPER CAR SEATS?	CHILDREN'S REACTION TO LEAVING OTHER PARTY

DETAILS:

DETAILS:

DETAILS:

DETAILS:

DETAILS:

CHILDREN'S RETURN

MONTH OF:					
DATE	WHO	LATE OR NO SHOW	ISSUES DURING DROP OFF	PROPER CAR SEATS?	CHILDREN'S REACTION TO LEAVING OTHER PARTY

DETAILS:

DETAILS:

DETAILS:

DETAILS:

DETAILS:

CHILDREN'S RETURN

MONTH OF:					
DATE	**WHO**	**LATE OR NO SHOW**	**ISSUES DURING DROP OFF**	**PROPER CAR SEATS?**	**CHILDREN'S REACTION TO LEAVING OTHER PARTY**

DETAILS:

DETAILS:

DETAILS:

DETAILS:

DETAILS:

FASTEN PICTURES OF CHILDREN'S RETURN APPEARANCE; DATE THE BACK OF EACH PICTURE

FASTEN PICTURES OF CHILDREN'S RETURN
APPEARANCE; DATE THE BACK OF EACH PICTURE

FASTEN PICTURES OF CHILDREN'S RETURN APPEARANCE; DATE THE BACK OF EACH PICTURE

VISIT DETAILS

MONTH OF:					
DATE	CHILD'S NAME	ILLNESS OR INJURIES	ITEMS NOT RETURNED OR BROKEN	PROPER FITTING CLEAN CLOTHING	BROKEN PROMISES OR MISSED CELEBRATIONS

DETAILS:

DETAILS:

DETAILS:

DETAILS:

VISIT DETAILS

MONTH OF:					
DATE	CHILD'S NAME	ILLNESS OR INJURIES	ITEMS NOT RETURNED OR BROKEN	PROPER FITTING CLEAN CLOTHING	BROKEN PROMISES OR MISSED CELEBRATIONS

DETAILS:

DETAILS:

DETAILS:

DETAILS:

VISIT DETAILS

MONTH OF:					
DATE	CHILD'S NAME	ILLNESS OR INJURIES	ITEMS NOT RETURNED OR BROKEN	PROPER FITTING CLEAN CLOTHING	BROKEN PROMISES OR MISSED CELEBRATIONS

DETAILS:

DATE	CHILD'S NAME	ILLNESS OR INJURIES	ITEMS NOT RETURNED OR BROKEN	PROPER FITTING CLEAN CLOTHING	BROKEN PROMISES OR MISSED CELEBRATIONS

DETAILS:

DATE	CHILD'S NAME	ILLNESS OR INJURIES	ITEMS NOT RETURNED OR BROKEN	PROPER FITTING CLEAN CLOTHING	BROKEN PROMISES OR MISSED CELEBRATIONS

DETAILS:

DATE	CHILD'S NAME	ILLNESS OR INJURIES	ITEMS NOT RETURNED OR BROKEN	PROPER FITTING CLEAN CLOTHING	BROKEN PROMISES OR MISSED CELEBRATIONS

DETAILS:

VISIT DETAILS

MONTH OF:					
DATE	CHILD'S NAME	ILLNESS OR INJURIES	ITEMS NOT RETURNED OR BROKEN	PROPER FITTING CLEAN CLOTHING	BROKEN PROMISES OR MISSED CELEBRATIONS

DETAILS:

DETAILS:

DETAILS:

DETAILS:

CHILDREN'S MONTHLY ACCOMPLISHMENTS

DATE	CHILD'S NAME	ACCOMPLISHMENT TYPE (ACADEMIC, SOCIAL, EXTRA-CURRICULER...)	CLUB, AWARD TITLE	ADVISE OTHER PARENT? IF YES, WHAT METHOD?	DID PARENT ATTEND OR CALL CHILD?

(Insert Date)

Re: (Other Parent's Name)

(Insert Your Name)
(Insert Street Address)
(Insert Street Address)
(Insert Phone Number)

(Insert Requesting Agency)
Central Records Division
(Insert Agency's Street Address)
(Insert Agency's Street Address)

To (Insert Agency Name) Central Records:

We are writing to request all offense records on (insert name including DOB) from (recommend 6 month increments) Please also include all assistance calls for address:

(Insert other parent's address here)

We can be reached at (insert your phone number). We appreciate your time and quick response.

Sincerely,

(Your signature)

(Your Name)

PERIODIC PUBLIC RECORD REQUEST

DATE	REPORTING AGENCY (911, POLICE REPORTS, CLERK OF COURTS)	TYPE OF REPORT (CIVIL, DOMESTIC, CRIMINAL)	PERSONS INVOLVED	ANY CRIMINAL CHARGES FILED	REPORT DETAILS

ATTACH REPORTS HERE

ATTACH REPORTS HERE

ADDITIONAL NOTES PAGE FOR MONTH:

ADDITIONAL NOTES PAGE FOR MONTH:

ADDITIONAL NOTES PAGE FOR MONTH:

_____

_____

_____

_____

_____

_____

_____

_____

_____

_____

_____

_____

_____

_____

_____

_____

_____

_____

_____

_____

_____

_____

_____

2013

JANUARY

S	M	T	W	T	F	S
		1	2	3	4	5
6	7	8	9	10	11	12
13	14	15	16	17	18	19
20	21	22	23	24	25	26
27	28	29	30	31		

FEBRUARY

S	M	T	W	T	F	S
					1	2
3	4	5	6	7	8	9
10	11	12	13	14	15	16
17	18	19	20	21	22	23
24	25	26	27	28		

MARCH

S	M	T	W	T	F	S
					1	2
3	4	5	6	7	8	9
10	11	12	13	14	15	16
17	18	19	20	21	22	23
24	25	26	27	28	29	30
31						

APRIL

S	M	T	W	T	F	S
	1	2	3	4	5	6
7	8	9	10	11	12	13
14	15	16	17	18	19	20
21	22	23	24	25	26	27
28	29	30				

MAY

S	M	T	W	T	F	S
			1	2	3	4
5	6	7	8	9	10	11
12	13	14	15	16	17	18
19	20	21	22	23	24	25
26	27	28	29	30	31	

JUNE

S	M	T	W	T	F	S
						1
2	3	4	5	6	7	8
9	10	11	12	13	14	15
16	17	18	19	20	21	22
23	24	25	26	27	28	29
30						

JULY

S	M	T	W	T	F	S
	1	2	3	4	5	6
7	8	9	10	11	12	13
14	15	16	17	18	19	20
21	22	23	24	25	26	27
28	29	30	31			

AUGUST

S	M	T	W	T	F	S
				1	2	3
4	5	6	7	8	9	10
11	12	13	14	15	16	17
18	19	20	21	22	23	24
25	26	27	28	29	30	31

SEPTEMBER

S	M	T	W	T	F	S
1	2	3	4	5	6	7
8	9	10	11	12	13	14
15	16	17	18	19	20	21
22	23	24	25	26	27	28
29	30					

OCTOBER

S	M	T	W	T	F	S
		1	2	3	4	5
6	7	8	9	10	11	12
13	14	15	16	17	18	19
20	21	22	23	24	25	26
27	28	29	30	31		

NOVEMBER

S	M	T	W	T	F	S
					1	2
3	4	5	6	7	8	9
10	11	12	13	14	15	16
17	18	19	20	21	22	23
24	25	26	27	28	29	30

DECEMBER

S	M	T	W	T	F	S
1	2	3	4	5	6	7
8	9	10	11	12	13	14
15	16	17	18	19	20	21
22	23	24	25	26	27	28
29	30	31				

2014

JANUARY

S	M	T	W	T	F	S
			1	2	3	4
5	6	7	8	9	10	11
12	13	14	15	16	17	18
19	20	21	22	23	24	25
26	27	28	29	30	31	

FEBRUARY

S	M	T	W	T	F	S
						1
2	3	4	5	6	7	8
9	10	11	12	13	14	15
16	17	18	19	20	21	22
23	24	25	26	27	28	

MARCH

S	M	T	W	T	F	S
						1
2	3	4	5	6	7	8
9	10	11	12	13	14	15
16	17	18	19	20	21	22
23	24	25	26	27	28	29
30	31					

APRIL

S	M	T	W	T	F	S
		1	2	3	4	5
6	7	8	9	10	11	12
13	14	15	16	17	18	19
20	21	22	23	24	25	26
27	28	29	30			

MAY

S	M	T	W	T	F	S
				1	2	3
4	5	6	7	8	9	10
11	12	13	14	15	16	17
18	19	20	21	22	23	24
25	26	27	28	29	30	31

JUNE

S	M	T	W	T	F	S
1	2	3	4	5	6	7
8	9	10	11	12	13	14
15	16	17	18	19	20	21
22	23	24	25	26	27	28
29	30					

JULY

S	M	T	W	T	F	S
		1	2	3	4	5
6	7	8	9	10	11	12
13	14	15	16	17	18	19
20	21	22	23	24	25	26
27	28	29	30	31		

AUGUST

S	M	T	W	T	F	S
					1	2
3	4	5	6	7	8	9
10	11	12	13	14	15	16
17	18	19	20	21	22	23
24	25	26	27	28	29	30
31						

SEPTEMBER

S	M	T	W	T	F	S
	1	2	3	4	5	6
7	8	9	10	11	12	13
14	15	16	17	18	19	20
21	22	23	24	25	26	27
28	29	30				

OCTOBER

S	M	T	W	T	F	S
			1	2	3	4
5	6	7	8	9	10	11
12	13	14	15	16	17	18
19	20	21	22	23	24	25
26	27	28	29	30	31	

NOVEMBER

S	M	T	W	T	F	S
						1
2	3	4	5	6	7	8
9	10	11	12	13	14	15
16	17	18	19	20	21	22
23	24	25	26	27	28	29
30						

DECEMBER

S	M	T	W	T	F	S
	1	2	3	4	5	6
7	8	9	10	11	12	13
14	15	16	17	18	19	20
21	22	23	24	25	26	27
28	29	30	31			

Made in the USA
Monee, IL
31 July 2022

10630198R00118